BROOKE SHIELDS:
From Child Star to Icon

Jerry.C.Smith

TABLE OF CONTENTS

From Child star to Icon

INTRODUCTION:

"In world of entertainment, few stories captivate as profoundly as that of Brooke Shields. From her humble beginnings as a child star to her enduring status as an iconic figure, Brooke's journey through the glitz and glamour of Hollywood has been one of both triumph and tribulation. This biography delves deep into the life and career of a young girl who captured hearts on screen and grew to become a cultural symbol of resilience and grace. Join us on a captivating exploration of the highs, lows, and indelible legacy of the incomparable Brooke Shields.

CHAPTER 1:WHO IS BROOKE SHIELDS:

Brooke Shields is an American actress and model known for her extensive work in film, television, and modelling. She gained prominence in the 1980s for her roles in films such as "The Blue Lagoon" and "Endless Love." Additionally, she has appeared in various TV shows, including the long-running series "Suddenly Susan." Besides her acting career, Shields has also been recognized for her contributions to fashion and her advocacy work in support of women's issues and mental health awareness.

1.1:A Glimpse into a Promising Future:

As a young star on the rise, Brooke Shields exuded an aura of promise and potential that transcended her age. Her captivating presence on screen and in the public eye hinted at a future brimming with endless possibilities. With her charming innocence and undeniable talent, she quickly became a household name, capturing the hearts of audiences worldwide. This chapter in Brooke's life serves as a testament to the beginnings of a journey that would ultimately redefine the landscape of stardom and leave an indelible mark on the realms of entertainment and advocacy.

1.2:The Early Years:

During the early years of Brooke Shields, a star was born, setting the stage for a remarkable journey through the realm of show business. With an innate charm and undeniable charisma, Shields stepped into the spotlight at a tender age, captivating audiences with her natural talent and endearing presence. Her introduction to the world of entertainment paved the way for an extraordinary career that would see her rise to prominence as a celebrated child star. Despite the challenges and complexities that often accompany early fame, Brooke Shields' formative years laid the foundation for a lasting legacy that transcends generations.

1.3:Background:

Brooke Shields was born on May 31, 1965, in New York City, USA, to a family deeply involved in the world of entertainment and academia. Her mother, Teri Shields, played a pivotal role in her early career, acting as both a manager and a guiding force. With her father, Francis Alexander Shields, working as a businessman and a Revlon executive, Brooke grew up in an environment that fostered both creativity and ambition. This unique blend of artistic exposure and business acumen shaped her early worldview, laying the groundwork for a multifaceted career that would span various industries, from fashion to film and beyond.

1.4:Family:

Brooke Shields comes from a closely knit and influential family. Her parents, Francis Alexander Shields and Teri Shields, provided her with a nurturing environment that fostered her burgeoning talent and ambition.
Additionally, she has two stepbrothers, Olympia and Marina, from her father's second marriage. In 1997, Brooke married tennis legend Andre Agassi, though they later divorced in 1999. Subsequently, she married Chris

From Child star to Icon

Henchy, a television writer and producer, with whom she has two daughters. Shields' strong family ties have played a significant role in shaping her personal and professional life, providing a stable foundation amid the ever-changing landscape of the entertainment industry.

CHAPTER 2:ENTERING THE SPOTLIGHT:

Entering the spotlight at a young age, Brooke Shields swiftly captured the attention of the entertainment industry and the public alike. Her breakthrough role in the controversial film "Pretty Baby" in 1978 marked her emergence as a rising star, showcasing her remarkable acting abilities and commanding on-screen presence. With her modelling career taking off concurrently, she became a prominent figure in the fashion world, gracing the covers of numerous magazines and solidifying her status as an influential icon. Brooke Shields' early foray into the limelight set the stage for a dynamic and enduring presence in both Hollywood and the world of fashion.

2.1:Hollywood's Darling:

During her early career, Brooke Shields earned the moniker "Hollywood's Darling" as she became a much sought-after talent in the film industry. Her roles in notable movies such as "The Blue Lagoon" and "Endless Love" solidified her status as a leading actress and an influential figure in popular culture. With her striking looks and undeniable screen presence, Shields captured the hearts of audiences worldwide, earning critical acclaim and widespread admiration. Her magnetic performances and undeniable charm further solidified her position as one of the most recognizable faces in Hollywood, propelling her to the forefront of the entertainment industry in the 1980s.

2.2:Challenges:

Throughout her career, Brooke Shields faced a series of challenges that tested her resilience and determination. Managing the transition from child stardom to adult roles, she encountered hurdles in redefining her public image and expanding her acting repertoire. Moreover, navigating the intense media scrutiny and public pressure posed additional obstacles, requiring her to navigate personal and professional challenges under the relentless gaze of the spotlight. Despite these adversities, Shields persisted, demonstrating a remarkable strength of character and an unwavering commitment to her craft, ultimately emerging as a symbol of endurance and grace in the face of adversity.

2.3:Controversies in Early Career:

During the early stages of her career, Brooke Shields encountered controversies that drew significant public attention. Her roles in controversial films, including "Pretty Baby" and "The Blue Lagoon," sparked debates about the boundaries of child actors in mature roles. Additionally, her appearances in provocative advertising campaigns stirred discussions about the portrayal of adolescent sexuality in the media. These controversies not only tested Shields' resolve but also prompted broader conversations about the intersection of fame, youth, and societal norms. Despite the challenges, Shields navigated these early controversies with poise, further solidifying her status as a resilient and multifaceted figure in the entertainment industry.

CHAPTER 3:TRANSITIONING TO ADULTHOOD:

As Brooke Shields transitioned from her early years as a child star to adulthood, she embarked on a transformative journey both personally and professionally. Her deliberate shift towards more mature roles in films and television showcased her versatility as an actress, allowing her to explore complex and nuanced characters. Alongside her acting career, Shields successfully ventured into other arenas, including modelling, where she continued to leave an indelible mark on the fashion industry. This period of transition marked a significant chapter in Shields' life, highlighting her adaptability and persistence in navigating the challenges of growing up in the public eye.

3.1:Career:

Brooke Shields' illustrious career spans decades and encompasses diverse roles in film, television, and modelling. From her breakthrough performances in films like "Pretty Baby" and "The Blue Lagoon" to her acclaimed television work in shows such as "Suddenly Susan" and "Lipstick Jungle," Shields has consistently demonstrated her range and talent as an actress. Additionally, her successful foray into the world of fashion modelling, marked by collaborations with renowned designers and brands, further solidified her status as an influential figure in the industry. Shields' multifaceted career trajectory reflects her enduring impact and versatility in the realms of entertainment and fashion.

3.2:Personal Milestones:

Throughout her life, Brooke Shields has achieved significant personal milestones that have shaped her journey and contributed to her enduring legacy. From earning a degree in French Literature from Princeton University to balancing the demands of motherhood with her thriving career, Shields has demonstrated her commitment to personal growth and familial values. Her advocacy for women's health issues and her dedication to promoting mental health awareness have also marked important milestones in her personal and philanthropic endeavours. Brooke Shields' unwavering dedication to personal and social causes has solidified her position as not only an accomplished artist but also a compassionate and influential public figure.

3.3:Successes:

Brooke Shields has experienced a multitude of successes throughout her career, each contributing to her enduring prominence in the world of entertainment. From her early achievements as a renowned child star to her acclaimed performances in a diverse range of films and television shows, Shields has consistently garnered praise for her talent and versatility. Her endeavours in the fashion industry, including high-profile modelling campaigns and collaborations, have further solidified her status as a style icon. Beyond her professional accomplishments, Shields' advocacy work, particularly in the fields of women's health and mental wellness, has earned her widespread recognition and respect. Her enduring successes reflect not only her exceptional talent but also her commitment to making a positive impact on society.

3.4:Struggles:

Brooke Shields has faced various struggles throughout her life and career, navigating the complexities of fame and public scrutiny with resilience and determination. From managing the pressures of early stardom and the challenges of transitioning to adult roles to balancing personal and professional demands, Shields has grappled with the inherent complexities of the entertainment industry. Moreover, her candid discussions about postpartum depression and her advocacy for mental health awareness underscore the personal struggles she has overcome, highlighting her courage and vulnerability. Despite these challenges, Brooke Shields' unwavering spirit and openness about her experiences have resonated with audiences worldwide, cementing her status as an enduring and relatable figure in the public eye.

CHAPTER 4:PERSONAL LIFE:

Brooke Shields' personal life has been marked by significant relationships, milestones, and a steadfast commitment to her family. Her marriage to tennis legend Andre Agassi and subsequent marriage to television writer and producer Chris Henchy have been key aspects of her personal narrative. Alongside her romantic relationships, her experiences as a devoted mother to her two daughters have played a central role in her life. Shields' emphasis on maintaining a strong familial foundation amidst the demands of a thriving career reflects her dedication to nurturing meaningful connections and fostering a balanced personal life.

4.1:Relationships:

Brooke Shields' relationships have been a prominent aspect of her personal life, capturing the attention of the public and the media. Her high-profile marriage to tennis champion Andre Agassi, which garnered significant public interest, reflected a dynamic union of two influential figures in the world of sports and entertainment. Following her divorce from Agassi, Shields found love and companionship in her relationship with Chris Henchy, a successful television writer and producer. Their enduring partnership has showcased a shared commitment to family and mutual support, underscoring the importance of strong personal connections in Shields' life journey.

4.2:Maintaining Relevance in a Changing Industry:

In the ever-evolving landscape of the entertainment industry, Brooke Shields has demonstrated an exceptional ability to adapt and maintain relevance across various platforms. With her notable presence in both film and television, Shields has embraced diverse roles that showcase her versatility as an actress. Moreover, her continued engagement in the world of fashion and her active participation in philanthropic endeavours have further solidified her status as a multifaceted and influential figure. Shields' enduring relevance serves as a testament to her enduring talent, adaptability, and unwavering dedication to her craft,

From Child star to Icon

positioning her as a timeless icon in the realm of entertainment and beyond.

CHAPTER 5:THE ICON EMERGES:

As her career progressed, Brooke Shields emerged as an iconic figure, revered for her contributions to the realms of entertainment, fashion, and advocacy. Her compelling performances in critically acclaimed films and television shows solidified her status as a respected actress, while her influential presence in the fashion world cemented her position as a style icon. Shields' unwavering commitment to social causes, including her advocacy for women's health and mental wellness, further elevated her status as a role model and a beacon of empowerment. Her multifaceted contributions to popular culture have positioned her as an enduring and influential figure, transcending the boundaries of the entertainment industry and leaving an indelible legacy.

5.1:Impact on Pop Culture:

Brooke Shields' impact on pop culture has been profound and enduring, shaping trends and sparking conversations that have resonated across generations. Her early prominence as a child star and her subsequent evolution into an influential actress and model set the stage for a dynamic cultural shift, redefining the standards of beauty and success in the entertainment industry. Shields' trailblazing presence in the world of fashion, coupled with her candid discussions about mental health and women's issues, has inspired a generation of individuals to embrace their uniqueness and prioritise holistic well-being. Her enduring influence on pop culture continues to transcend traditional boundaries, leaving an indelible mark on the fabric of societal norms and perceptions.

5.2:Public Advocacy:

Brooke Shields' public advocacy efforts have extended beyond the realms of entertainment and fashion, encompassing a diverse range of social causes and initiatives. Her vocal advocacy for women's health issues, including her open discussions about postpartum depression, has brought crucial attention to often stigmatised topics, fostering meaningful conversations and promoting awareness. Additionally, her active involvement in mental health advocacy has highlighted the importance of destigmatizing conversations around emotional well-being and seeking support. Shields' dedication to using her platform for social good underscores her commitment to fostering positive change and creating a more empathetic and inclusive society.

5.3:Charity Work:

Brooke Shields' philanthropic endeavours have encompassed a wide range of charitable causes, reflecting her dedication to making a positive impact on society. Her involvement in various charitable organisations focused on women's health, children's welfare, and mental wellness has served as a catalyst for meaningful change and advocacy. Shields' active participation in fundraising events and her role as a spokesperson for numerous charitable initiatives have helped raise awareness and support for critical societal issues. Her commitment to leveraging her influence for the betterment of communities has solidified her reputation as a compassionate and dedicated advocate for those in need.

CHAPTER 6:BEYOND ACTING:

In addition to her successful acting career, Brooke Shields has ventured into various creative and entrepreneurial pursuits, showcasing her multifaceted talents beyond the realm of acting. Her foray into the world of fashion modelling, characterised by collaborations with esteemed designers and iconic brands, has solidified her status as a revered style icon. Furthermore, her forays into writing, including the publication of books and memoirs, have highlighted her aptitude for storytelling and self-expression. Shields' diverse ventures beyond acting underscore her versatility and creative acumen, further solidifying her position as a dynamic and influential figure in the realms of entertainment, fashion, and literature.

6.1:Exploring Brooke's Entrepreneurial Ventures:

Brooke Shields' entrepreneurial ventures encompass a diverse range of creative and business endeavours, showcasing her versatility and business acumen. Her collaborations with prominent fashion brands and designers have not only solidified her status as a style icon but have also highlighted her keen eye for design and aesthetics. Additionally, her forays into writing and publishing, including the release of books and memoirs, have showcased her talent for storytelling and self-expression. Shields' entrepreneurial spirit, coupled with her creative vision, has positioned her as a dynamic force in both the entertainment and business worlds, solidifying her legacy as a multifaceted and influential figure.

6.2:Self expression :

Brooke Shields' journey of self-expression has been characterised by her multifaceted talents and creative pursuits across various artistic mediums. From her acclaimed performances in film and television to her endeavours in fashion modelling and writing, Shields has consistently used her platform to convey her unique perspective and voice. Her openness about personal experiences, including her struggles with mental health, has further underscored her commitment to authentic storytelling and fostering meaningful connections with her audience. Shields' unwavering dedication to self-expression has not only shaped her artistic trajectory but has also inspired a sense of empowerment and empathy among her global fan base.

6.3:Empowerment:

Brooke Shields' journey has been defined by her unwavering commitment to empowerment, both in her personal and professional life. Through her advocacy for women's health issues and her candid discussions about mental wellness, she has encouraged open dialogue and destigmatized conversations surrounding sensitive topics. Additionally, her multifaceted career, marked by her successes in film, television, fashion, and writing, serves as a testament to her resilience and determination. Shields' advocacy for self-expression and her dedication to using her platform for social good have inspired countless individuals to embrace their authenticity and prioritise holistic well-being, cementing her legacy as a beacon of empowerment and resilience.

CHAPTER 7:CAREER RESURGENCE:

Brooke Shields' career resurgence marked a dynamic chapter in her professional trajectory, characterised by a renewed presence in both the entertainment and fashion industries. Her notable roles in acclaimed television shows and films, along with her impactful collaborations with leading fashion designers and brands, reinvigorated her status as a prominent figure in popular culture. Moreover, her continued engagement in philanthropic initiatives and advocacy work further solidified her legacy as a multifaceted and influential public figure. Shields' career resurgence stands as a testament to her enduring talent, adaptability, and unwavering commitment to using her platform for positive change and empowerment.

7.1:Diverse Ventures:

Brooke Shields' diverse ventures encompass a broad spectrum of creative and entrepreneurial pursuits that highlight her multifaceted talents and interests. From her successful acting career in film and television to her influential presence in the fashion industry, Shields has demonstrated a dynamic range of skills and capabilities. Moreover, her endeavours in writing and publishing, including the release of books and memoirs, showcase her aptitude for storytelling and self-expression. Shields' diverse ventures underscore her versatility and creative vision, solidifying her reputation as a dynamic and influential figure across multiple industries.

7.2:Personal Life in the Public Eye:

Brooke Shields' personal life has often been subject to public interest and scrutiny, with her relationships and family dynamics garnering significant attention. Her high-profile marriages to notable figures in the entertainment industry and her experiences as a devoted mother have been frequent topics of media coverage. Shields' openness about her personal struggles, including her battles with postpartum depression, has fostered important conversations about mental health and well-being. Despite the challenges of living in the public eye, Shields has maintained a sense of grace and authenticity, offering a relatable and human perspective

From Child star to Icon

on the complexities of personal relationships and the demands of fame.

CHAPTER 8:REFLECTIONS ON FAME:

Throughout her career, Brooke Shields has offered insightful reflections on the complexities and implications of fame. Her candid discussions about the challenges of growing up in the public eye and navigating the pressures of the entertainment industry have provided a nuanced perspective on the realities of celebrity status. Shields' introspective musings on the balance between personal identity and public persona have underscored the importance of maintaining authenticity and integrity in the face of widespread recognition. Her reflections on fame serve as a poignant reminder of the human experience behind the glamour and glitz, offering valuable insights into the intricacies of maintaining a sense of self in the spotlight.

8.1:Media Scrutiny:

Brooke Shields has faced substantial media scrutiny throughout her career, with her personal life and professional endeavours often subject to intense public interest. Her relationships, family dynamics, and personal struggles have been frequent topics of tabloid speculation, placing her under the relentless gaze of the media spotlight. Shields' ability to navigate the complexities of fame and media scrutiny with grace and resilience has offered a compelling narrative of strength and perseverance. Despite the challenges posed by heightened public attention, Shields has remained steadfast in her commitment to authenticity and self-empowerment, serving as an inspiring example of resilience in the face of relentless media scrutiny.

8.2:Impact in people's Life:

Brooke Shields' impact on people's lives has been profound and far-reaching, extending beyond her contributions to the entertainment industry. Her candid discussions about personal struggles, including postpartum depression and mental health, have resonated with individuals worldwide, fostering a sense of empathy and understanding. Moreover, her advocacy for women's health and her commitment to philanthropic initiatives have inspired countless individuals to prioritise their well-being and contribute to meaningful causes. Shields' enduring influence as a role model and advocate has left an indelible mark on the lives of those who have found solace and inspiration in her story, solidifying her legacy as a beacon of resilience and empowerment.

CHAPTER 9:LEGACY:

Brooke Shields' legacy is characterised by her multifaceted contributions to the realms of entertainment, fashion, and advocacy. Her influential presence in film and television, coupled with her impactful modelling career, has left an indelible mark on popular culture, reshaping the standards of beauty and success in the industry. Moreover, her advocacy for mental health awareness and women's issues has fostered meaningful conversations and inspired positive change within communities. Shields' enduring legacy serves as a testament to her enduring talent, resilience, and dedication to empowering others, solidifying her position as a timeless and influential figure in the realms of entertainment and social advocacy.

9.1:Influence:

Brooke Shields' influence has transcended the boundaries of the entertainment industry, leaving an indelible mark on popular culture and societal norms. Her impact on the realms of fashion and beauty has redefined standards of elegance and grace, inspiring individuals to embrace their unique identities and celebrate diversity. Moreover, her candid discussions about personal struggles and her advocacy for mental health awareness have sparked important conversations, fostering empathy and understanding on a global scale. Shields' enduring influence as a role model and advocate has empowered individuals to prioritise their well-being and contribute to positive social change, cementing her status as a timeless and revered figure of inspiration.

9.2:Enduring Impact on Media:

Brooke Shields' enduring impact on the media landscape has been significant, reshaping the narrative surrounding fame, beauty, and personal struggles. Her notable presence in film, television, and fashion has redefined industry standards, highlighting the importance of authenticity and inclusivity in popular culture. Additionally, her advocacy for mental health awareness and women's issues has sparked crucial conversations, prompting a shift in the media's approach to sensitive topics. Shields' enduring impact on the media has contributed to a more empathetic and informed public discourse, reflecting her unwavering commitment to fostering positive change and empowerment within the industry and beyond.

9.3:Enduring Impact Society:

Brooke Shields' enduring impact on society has been far-reaching, extending beyond her contributions to the entertainment industry. Her advocacy for women's health issues and mental wellness has inspired individuals to prioritise holistic well-being and destigmatize important conversations surrounding emotional health. Moreover, her commitment to philanthropic initiatives and charitable causes has catalysed positive change within communities, fostering a culture of empathy and compassion. Shields' enduring impact on society reflects her dedication to using her platform for social good and her unwavering commitment to empowering individuals to embrace their authenticity and contribute to a more compassionate and inclusive world.

CONCLUSION:

In this illuminating journey through the life and career of Brooke Shields, we have witnessed the transformation of a young star into a cultural icon. From her early years as a child actress to her enduring impact on the realms of fashion, advocacy, and media, Shields' story embodies resilience, grace, and unwavering commitment to personal growth and social empowerment. Her journey through the ever-evolving landscape of fame and her steadfast dedication to using her platform for positive change have left an indelible mark on the fabric of popular culture and societal norms. As we bid farewell to this captivating narrative, we are reminded of the enduring legacy of a true icon, whose influence transcends generations and continues to inspire countless individuals to embrace their uniqueness and make a meaningful impact on the world around them.

From Child star to Icon

www.ingramcontent.com/pod-product-compliance
Lightning Source LLC
Chambersburg PA
CBHW072223290526
45794CB00007B/2870